Alice Burnet
from all.
Christmas. 1926

732·21
17

Alice Burnet
from all.
Christmas. 1926

732·21

PORTRAIT
MINIATURES

TEXT BY
Dr. GEORGE C. WILLIAMSON

EDITED BY
CHARLES HOLME

MCMX
'THE STUDIO' LTD.
LONDON, PARIS, NEW YORK

39245

PREFATORY NOTE.

The Author and Editor desire to express their grateful thanks to Fürst Franz Auersperg, Sir Charles Dilke, Bart., Dr. Figdor, Mr. E. M. Hodgkins, Lord Hothfield, Mr. J. Pierpont Morgan, Lady Maria Ponsonby, Mr. J. Ward Usher, Gräfin Emma Wilczck-Emo-Capodilista, and the anonymous collector, who have so kindly placed their treasures at their disposal, and permitted them to be illustrated in these pages.

ILLUSTRATIONS IN COLOUR.

ILLUSTRATIONS IN MONOTONE.

PORTRAIT MINIATURES. By
Dr. G. C. Williamson.

A RECENT French writer, in referring to the art of portrait painting, exalted it to the highest rank, proclaiming it the greatest of all arts. He then proceeded, by a series of curious antithetical sentences, to set forth his opinion of portrait painting, stating that it was at once the oldest and the most modern of arts, the easiest and the most difficult, the simplest and the most abstruse, the clearest and the most subtle. His statement, it is clear, contained a definite basis of truth, coupled with a certain interesting extravagance of expression. It is quite true that to draw a portrait was the aim of the very earliest of draughtsmen, whether it was that of his companion or of one of the beasts of chase, and whether he carved it on a bone, or daubed it on the wall of his dwelling. The first endeavour, also, of a child, playing with a pencil, or a brush, is to draw a portrait, and the very simplest outline does occasionally reveal that an idea of portraiture is latent in the mind of the young artist. If only simplicity of line is desired, nothing can be more simple, while at the same time nothing is more perfect, than the outline or profile drawing of such a great artist as Holbein, or the work of some of the early French draughtsmen.

At the same time, the subtlety of this draughtsmanship cannot be denied. For complexity and difficulty, portraiture takes a supreme place, and yet, on the other hand, as the Frenchman points out in his antithetical sentences, it is to a certain extent a simple art, and we all know artists who are able with a piece of chalk to suggest an even startling likeness which they would be quite unable to complete into the form of a perfect portrait. Many a painter thinks at first that portraiture is simple and easy, in fact he finds it so, but the older he grows, the more does he realise that the human features are complex in the extreme, and that the variations of expression make the difficulties in the task of portraying them enormous. From very early times, however, there has been a natural desire to have portraits of the persons about us, and to have these portraits in portable form ; hence, after a long succession of vicissitudes, has come the miniature.

It is perhaps as well, even though the statement has been made over and over again, to emphasize the fact that the actual word miniature has nothing whatever to do with the size of the portrait. We accept it, however, as implying that the portrait is of portable size, and we shall apply it to such a portrait as can lie in the palm of one's hand, ignoring the fact that the word was originally derived from " minium " or red lead, and has come down to us from the little portraits on illuminated manuscripts, outlined or bordered with lines of red. In two countries especially, the art of painting miniatures has flourished, England and France, and in these two countries there have been schools of miniature painters, and a succession of great exponents of the art, while in the other countries of Europe there have only been now and again painters who have devoted especial attention to this branch of their art, and have taken high position in it. It is more especially an English art, because, although for exquisite grace, charming colouring, and dainty conception, the works of the French miniature painters take a high rank, even they must yield the palm for representation of character to the greatest English painter of miniatures, Samuel Cooper. Moreover, in no country but England has there been such a long series of painters in miniature, extending from the sixteenth century down to comparatively recent times.

It has been the fashion to commence a survey of English miniature painters by reference to Holbein, and it is not altogether an unsatisfactory manner in which to start (although Holbein was not an Englishman), because so many of his best works were painted in this country. It must not, however, be forgotten that portrait painting was practised by native English artists in the early part, or at least in the middle, of the fifteenth century, and although we know very little indeed about these English painters, yet we have many works remaining which must be attributed to them.

It may, moreover, be stated generally that the predecessors and contemporaries of Holbein in miniature work were mostly of foreign extraction, although working in England ; such, for example, as Lavina Terlinck and Gwillym Stretes. We know, however, that certain fourteenth-century manuscripts were actually executed in England, by an English artist, and as an example of such work, Mr. Lionel Cust, in his preface to the English Portraiture Exhibition at the Burlington Fine Arts Club, points out the Salisbury Lectionarium, with the portrait of Lord Lovell as its frontispiece, representing him receiving the book from its maker, John Siferwas. He refers also to the even better known portrait of Chaucer, painted by Occlive on the manuscript now in the British Museum.

There is also no question that the actual art of portrait miniature, such as we understand it at the present day, arose from that of painting portraits on manuscripts, and, as we have already pointed out in another place, it may further be derived from the similar portraits attached to treaties and to documents handed over to ambassadors. The illumination of a portrait of Francis I. on the ratification of a treaty of peace with England, August 18th, 1527, is a case in point. It represents the French King in excellent fashion, delineating character as well as portraiture, and is the work

2

of a painter of no mean skill and discernment. Similar portraits of Henry VIII., and Philip and Mary, dated 1543 and 1556, and painted in England, are not of such a high character as is the one of Francis, but still are sufficient to enable us to regard them as true portraits, representative of the monarchs as they were. Who first, says Mr. Cust, cut out the portrait in miniature from an illumination, and inserted it in a jewelled or ivory case or picture-box, it is impossible to surmise, but such a caprice, once started, was likely quickly to become popular. Who first gave up the use of vellum for such portraits, and found that a playing card in use at that day was a more convenient material on which to paint, we also do not know ; nor who, again, stretched a very fine piece of vellum or chicken-skin upon the playing-card, and used that as his basis, but the earliest Elizabethan miniatures painted in England are done in one of these two methods.

Prominent amongst the names of the Tudor painters stands out that of Hans Holbein the younger, and in the art of composition it is doubtful whether any successor has equalled him in con-summate skill. The illustration which we are allowed to give from Mr. Pierpont Morgan's collection, and which represents *Mrs. Pemberton* (Plate I.), is one of the most astonishing works ever produced by a miniature painter. The figure is so perfectly composed, and so marvellously set within the small compass of the circle, while the modelling is so subtle and delicate, so refined, and distinguished by such perfection of line and economy of material that it is always a delight to regard it, and no portrait painter would be ashamed to say that he had learned many a lesson from the unerring skill with which this marvellous portrait is produced. It cannot be said that all Holbein's works are on as high a level as is this particular picture, but the two portraits in the possession of the Queen of Holland, one representing a young lady, and the other an older man ; the portrait of the painter in the possession of the Duke of Buccleuch ; the wonderful *Anne of Cleves* in the collection of the late Mr. George Salting ; and the companion one of Henry VIII. in Mr. Pierpont Morgan's cabinet, are all distinguished by the same perfection of draughtsmanship and skill of composition. In Holbein we have, therefore, a fitting master, from whom to start the long series of miniature painters, which in England extended away down to the beginning of the nineteenth century, or even perhaps a little later, and in his successor, Nicholas Hilliard, we find the first of the masters who was actually an Englishman born and bred.

From whom Hilliard learned his art it is impossible to tell. It would be most interesting could we decide if he ever came into contact with Holbein, and hardly less so were we able to determine that any other master first gave him lessons in this fascinating art. That he began painting as quite a boy constitutes almost our first fact respecting him, and that is proved by his own portrait at the age of thirteen, signed with the young painter's initials in the usual conjoined form, and dated 1550. Of his history we know that Hilliard was the son of a man who was the High Sheriff of Exeter in 1560, Richard Hilliard by name, and that his mother was Laurence, the daughter of John Wall, a goldsmith of London. The statement that the father became High Sheriff is authorised by the inscription on the case belonging to Lord De L'Isle which at one time contained a portrait of the father executed by the son, and Walpole gives us the information respecting Hilliard's mother, corroborated by the fact that the painter named his son Laurence after his own mother. We also know that he married twice, as the portrait of his first wife Alicia Brandon at the age of twenty-two is in the Duke of Buccleuch's collection, and the inscription upon it, evidently added by the painter after his wife's death, tells us that he married again. Who his second wife was we do not know, but it seems probable that he survived her, because she is not mentioned in his will, and in it he constitutes his son Laurence his sole heir and executor. He was always spoken of with great respect by his contemporaries, is styled "Gentleman" or "Mr.", and his illness in 1610 is carefully referred to in the State Papers ; while James I., when he gives him the Royal Warrant of painting, expressly styles him " our well-beloved Gentleman, Nicholas Hylliard." It seems probable that by trade he was originally a goldsmith, and his portraits show us that the craft of the goldsmith had exercised a great influence over his life. In his delicate miniature portraits Hilliard never forgot his original craft, and even went so far upon occasion as to introduce what was distinctly jeweller's work into the portraits themselves. There is, for example, an actual diamond, minute certainly, set in one of his portraits, and the raised work representing jewels in other portraits is wrought with such skill and delicacy that only a goldsmith could encompass it. We know that he took Holbein as his model, for he himself says so, but his work is very different from that of the great Swabian. It is ornamental and decorative, very delicate, and elaborate, but flat and shadowless, and altogether lacking in the marvellous subtle modelling which marks out the work of Holbein. It resembles, in fact, more nearly the work of the early illuminators. It seems probable that Hilliard was not only a skilful miniature painter, but also an actual working goldsmith, and responsible for many of the extraordinary frames in which his portraits were set. Miss Helen Farquhar has with great skill elaborated a theory

4

which tends to prove this, and which appeared in a recent issue of the "Numismatic Chronicle." Certain jewels and miniature cases have been in the past attributed to the artist, and the result of Miss Farquhar's investigation is to make it more clear that such attribution has been accurate. Hilliard painted Queen Elizabeth many times, and amongst our illustrations will be found a portrait of the Queen (Plate II.) from the cabinet of a well-known collector, which sets forth the artist's peculiar technique. We also present an interesting example from Mr. Pierpont Morgan's collection which has been called a portrait of *Mary Queen of Scots* (Plate III., No. 2). It is dated 1581, and is certainly one of the few portraits which seems to stand the test of comparison with the well-known drawing and miniature of Mary Stuart attributed to Clouet. It is undoubtedly the work of Hilliard, and of remarkable excellence, and takes its place amongst the more or less mysterious portraits bearing the name of the ill-fated Queen.

Hilliard died in 1619, and appears to have been succeeded in his royal appointments and his professional work by his son Laurence, whose paintings so closely resemble those of the father that it is not always easy to distinguish the work of the two men. Very few of Laurence Hilliard's works are signed ; there are two belonging to Earl Beauchamp, and one in the collection of Mr. Pierpont Morgan. The main feature of the son's work consists in the beauty of the caligraphy in the inscriptions around the portraits. It is clearer than the more formal handwriting of the father, but florid, full of exquisite curves and flourishes, and very elaborate, while the colour-scheme adopted by the son is distinctly richer and more varied than that used by the father, and the composition is not quite so rigid and hard as was that of Nicholas.

The two Hilliards were, however, succeeded by two far greater men—the Olivers. One of them, Isaac, the father, was certainly Nicholas Hilliard's pupil, as the fact is mentioned more than once in Haydock's preface to his translation of Lomazzo. It seems to be possible that some of Isaac Oliver's works were copies of those of his master, and copies so accurately executed that it is not quite easy to determine respecting them. In the cabinet of Mr. Pierpont Morgan there is, for example, a miniature of Arabella Stuart which came from Walpole's collection. It has always borne the name of Hilliard, and Walpole himself was careful in the attributions he gave to his portraits, but in the Rijks Museum at Amsterdam there are two other portraits of the same lady, one of which is stated to be signed under the frame with the initials of Isaac Oliver, and there are two more, even more closely resembling it, in the collection at Sherborne Castle. The Morgan portrait is very characteristic of

5

Hilliard, and the two in Amsterdam closely resemble it. Our suggestion for a solution of the difficulty is that the two Dutch portraits are early copies by Oliver from his master's work. Oliver was an extremely expert painter, and a far more clever man than Hilliard, for the pencil drawings of the painter and his wife, which belong to the Earl of Derby, reveal him as a draughtsman of consummate skill. He was probably of Huguenot descent, the son, it is believed, of a certain Peter Olivier (or Oliver), a native of Rouen, who was residing in London in 1571, and we may take it that his birth was in about 1566 ; his death occurred in 1617, and he was buried in the church of St. Anne's, Blackfriars.

Amongst our colour plates are two delightful portraits by him representing *Frederick, King of Bohemia, and his Wife*, who was known in England as the "Queen of Hearts," signed miniatures from the collection of Sir Charles Dilke (Plate IV., Nos. 2 and 3). In the monotone illustrations there appear two remarkable works by this painter from the collection of Mr. Pierpont Morgan. One represents *Philip II., King of Spain* (Plate III., No. 1), a fine portrait, set in an elaborate locket of rock-crystal and enamel work, upon the reverse of which is a representation of the Crucifixion in grisaille. This portrait has an interesting history, because it was given by the king to the Duke of Osuna, and acquired from the Osuna family, quite recently. It bears a motto which may roughly be translated "He who gives himself, gives not a little thing," words which are eminently characteristic of the pride of the Spanish monarch. The other portrait is of hardly less interest. It depicts *Queen Anne of Denmark* (Plate III., No. 3), who was painted over and over again by Isaac Oliver, and who can always be readily distinguished by the jewels which she wore on her elaborate high collar or ruff. Amongst them invariably appears a representation of a sea-horse or a dolphin. This may perhaps have some allusion to her Scandinavian ancestry, but, in any case, it was a favourite jewel with the queen, and hardly one of her portraits appears without it. Here, again, the case containing the miniature is of extraordinary importance, because there is good evidence for attributing it to George Heriot, who was goldsmith and jeweller to Anne of Denmark, and was the founder of the great hospital and school which still bear his name in Edinburgh, while to the present generation he is perhaps better remembered as a character in Sir Walter Scott's "Fortunes of Nigel," in which delightful work he appears as "Jingling Geordie." There are portraits of Oliver himself in existence, and a delightful one of his son, while amongst the collection of the Queen of Holland there is one that is said to represent his wife. The most notable series of the works of this

6

painter is perhaps that which is generally known as the Digby series. Walpole tells the story of the discovery of these miniatures. He says that they were in a garret in an old house in Wales, enclosed in ebony and ivory cases, and locked up in a wainscot box, in which they were as well preserved as though only just painted. He was greatly excited about them, and was able to secure the entire collection, first buying from one owner the greater part of the collection, and then securing by a second purchase the remainder from the lady who shared them with the other heir. They were all sold at his sale at Strawberry Hill, and some of the finest of the portraits passed into the collection of the late Baroness Burdett-Coutts, others went to Mr. Holford, and many back again to the Digby family, who would gladly have purchased the whole, but were unable to afford the prices paid by the Baroness Burdett-Coutts, then Miss Angela Coutts. One little portrait was bought by Mr. Wentworth Dilke, and now belongs to Sir Charles Dilke, it represents one of the sons of Sir Kenelm Digby, and is a charmingly graceful little work, by the kind permission of its owner illustrated in these pages (Plate IV., No. 1).

The work of Peter Oliver cannot readily be distinguished from that of the father, save for the signature, and is as worthy of praise in every respect, even if it is not more so. That of the father is a little sterner and more forcible than the work of the son, but Peter Oliver is not only known by his delightful miniatures, but also by the copies in miniature size and style which he prepared for Charles I., and which represented some of the great pictures in the King's collection. Several of these copies still remain at Windsor Castle, others are scattered in various collections, and in some instances they are of peculiar importance. For example, there is one in Mr. Pierpont Morgan's collection, representing the marriage of St. Catherine, by a Venetian painter, probably Titian or Palma Vecchio, which is apparently the only record of a vanished painting at one time in the King's collection, but later on sold into Spain, and which there perished in a fire at Seville.

A curious story is told by Horace Walpole concerning some miniatures by Peter Oliver. He says that Vertue handed down the information that Charles II. being very anxious to re-purchase the portraits which had been dispersed on the execution of his father, was told that the widow of Peter Oliver had taken back some of the miniatures, and had them in her possession. The King went to Isleworth to see her, disguising himself that he should not be known, and she showed him several works by her husband. He was pleased with them and tried to purchase them, but the lady stated that she was anxious to submit them to the King, and if he

7

did not buy them, a price should be named for their disposal. The King then discovered himself to her, and at once she showed him many more miniatures which she had not shown to anyone else, and King Charles desired to acquire them all. She would not, however, quote a price to him, but promised to look over her husband's books, and let His Majesty know what prices had been paid to Peter Oliver by Charles I. The King took away the miniatures with him, and afterwards sent one of the grooms of the bedchamber to Mrs. Oliver, offering her a thousand pounds for them, or an annuity of £300 for her life. She chose the latter, but after some few years, hearing that a great many of the miniatures had passed out of the King's possession, and had been given by him to the various ladies at the Court, Mrs. Oliver, who was given to express herself in somewhat blunt language, said that if she had thought the King would have given the miniatures to his mistresses and illegitimate children he should never have had them. Her remark, which was couched in very strong language, was carried by someone to the Court. The poor woman's annuity was at once stopped, and she never again received it.

Following Isaac and Peter Oliver in chronological survey, and necessarily omitting reference to some of the less important painters, we come to the name of a man of considerable eminence in his profession, John Hoskins. To a certain extent he has been over-shadowed by the extraordinary merit of his nephew and pupil, Samuel Cooper, but Hoskins was a very great painter himself, and his work marks the beginning of the broader and more powerful English miniature portraiture, as distinguished from the minute work of the men who had been trained under the influence of illuminators, and whose miniatures were too full of detail to be entirely satisfactory. There is no doubt that, as Walpole says, the carnations used in the faces painted by Hoskins are too bricky in colour, but the whole effect of the portrait is simple and dignified, and there is, for the first time in English minia-ture portraiture, a nobility of treatment and a sober grandeur of effect, extraordinarily impressive. The portrait of the *Duke of Buckingham* (Plate V.) from a well-known collection, illustrated in colour, well sets forth the dignity of Hoskins' works. It is an exceedingly fine miniature, quiet in colouring, and entirely satisfactory in composition. It is signed and dated, and, with respect to the signatures on miniatures by Hoskins, a few words must be said. It is well also to mark that in the works of Hoskins appears for the first time the division of the background, which is rather a notable feature in the portraits of Cooper, who evidently derived the idea from his uncle. The effect of this division on the lighting of the

8

portrait is excellent, the sitter being placed near to a window, by which hangs a curtain, and the window commanding a view which in many cases was adapted by the artist to some event in the history of the sitter. As regards the signatures Hoskins adopted several methods of signing his miniatures, combining his two initials in different forms of monogram, or separating them with or without the addition of the abbreviation " fc." Until quite recently the statement made by Vertue that Hoskins had a son, was incapable of proof; although the fact that the contemporary inscriptions on some of the miniatures at Ham House speak of " Old Hoskins," implies that there must have been a younger man of the same name, and it was thought that the variety of signatures might help clear up the doubtful question, and that perhaps the father adopted a certain method of signing his portraits, and the son another form of signature. Fortunately, however, in the collection of Mr. Pierpont Morgan, there appears a portrait of the Duke of Berwick, signed with conjoined initials, and bearing upon it an inscription, stating not only who it represented, but actually when it was painted. This miniature proved to contain the missing link of evidence, because there was no question about its authenticity, its accurate attribution, or its signature, but as it was painted in 1700, while we know that the elder Hoskins was buried in 1664, we have in it definite information, not only of the existence of the son, but of the fact that he was painting miniatures thirty-six years after his father had died. The same notable collection contains many works by the elder Hoskins, but only this one which can be definitely attributed to his son. The collections at Ham House and Montagu House are very rich in works by Hoskins, those at the former place being distinguished by delightful contemporary inscriptions on the backs of almost every portrait, recording in many instances the price paid to the artist for it. Of the works at Montagu House, one of the finest represents Charles II. in his youth, and in the collection at Ham is perhaps the largest work which Hoskins ever painted.

A particularly good example of the work of this master is the portrait of *Queen Henrietta Maria* (Plate VI.) from the Pierpont Morgan collection, and this miniature is the more interesting because apparently it has never been re-framed, for not only is the metal frame the contemporary one, but it possesses its original bevelled glass, the oval divided into a series of curved segments, each of which has its polished bevelled edge. Waller, in 1625, spoke of the Queen in these words:—

" Such a complexion and such radiant eyes,
Such lovely motions and such sharp replies,
Beyond our reach, and yet within our sight,
What envious power has placed this glorious light ?"

We need not, perhaps, accept the praises of the poet, but at least we may admire the quiet sweetness of the Queen's face in this charming portrait, and recognise the skill and dexterity with which it is delineated.

Trained and educated by Hoskins was Samuel Cooper, pre-eminently the greatest miniature painter that England ever produced, and in the opinion of many critics the noblest miniature painter of Europe. We know comparatively little about Cooper's history, but there are few artists concerning whom it would be more desirable to have information. Fortunately, Pepys mentions him several times in his wonderful diary; especially with reference to the portrait of Mrs. Pepys which her husband commissioned. He was evidently a great admirer of the work of Cooper, although, as regards this particular portrait, he does not appear to have been perfectly satisfied with the likeness. He says he was not " satisfied in the greatness of the resemblance, nor in the blue garment, but it was most certainly a most rare piece of work as to the painting," and he tells us the exact price that Cooper charged him, and adds that he sent him the money that night that he might be out of debt. Aubrey calls Cooper " the prince of limners of his age." Ray the naturalist, in writing to Aubrey, refers to a miniature portrait presented to the Ashmolean Museum as " a noble present and a thing of great value." Evelyn calls him " the rare limner " and describes the visit which he paid to the King's private room, where he found Cooper at work painting the royal portrait, and had the honour to hold the candle while it was being done, as Cooper, he says, " chose the night and candle-light for better finding out the shadows." To all this chorus of praise Walpole adds his voice, and tells us that, in his opinion, Cooper's works were so fine that they were perfect nature, and that if " a glass could expand Cooper's pictures to the size of Vandyck's, they would appear to have been painted for that proportion," adding that " if the Cooper portrait of Cromwell could be so enlarged, I do not know but Vandyck would appear less great by the comparison." Even with this criticism, Walpole is careful not to be entirely eulogistic, and he points out with unerring discrimination that, although the heads in Cooper's portraits were so fine, he yet possessed a lack of skill in draughtsmanship where other portions of the body were concerned, and, especially as regards the hands, he had a curious want of grace and accuracy, His faces, however, are superb, and well deserve all the praise that can be given to them. They have been called noble and masterly. and the words are befitting. The two portraits representing *Charles II.* and *The Earl of Loudoun,* which we present from the

10

Pierpont Morgan collection (Plate VII.), and the two in colour, depicting *Colonel Lilburne* and *Lady Fauconberg*, from the collection of Mr. Hodgkins (Plate VIII.), will well set forth the dignity and power possessed by this great master. His largest miniature is the portrait of Charles I. at Goodwood, and there is a somewhat smaller replica by the master's own hand in the Rijks Museum at Amsterdam. The Earl of Exeter possesses one of his rare half-length portraits, depicting Elizabeth, Countess of Devonshire, as a girl, and in the Victoria and Albert Museum is a large square portrait of the painter, by himself. With these exceptions, the majority of Cooper's works are ovals, varying in size, representing the head and shoulders only, and almost all the great collections of miniatures possess examples by the painter. As a rule, his colours have stood extraordinarily well ; in some instances, however, they have faded, but it has generally been owing to damp or to indifferent treatment on the part of the owners of the portraits. In Mr. Pierpont Morgan's collection one miniature representing *Lord Loudoun* (Plate VII., No. 2) is in extraordinarily perfect condition, but for a couple of generations it was lost sight of behind some oak panelling and has only recently come to light. Another very fine one, in the same collection, represents *Charles II.* (Plate VII., No. 1). Cooper's method of painting is very interesting, and as he has left behind several unfinished portraits, we are enabled to study it with considerable accuracy. It is clear that he commenced to draw the head and figure in brown, and, as a recent writer has pointed out, painted in the shadows with transparent sienna, and the half-tones with a pure grey blue. His work is executed upon vellum as a rule, but sometimes upon cardboard, and his flesh tints are nearly always transparent, although occasionally they are upon a white background, and in some few rare instances, where he desired special effect, he used opaque colours. Several of his portraits he has never carried beyond the early stages. They are only sketches, but such sketches as no one else could have done, exquisitely rendered, full of palpitating life. This is especially the case with the portrait of the Duke of Albemarle at Windsor, and with one in the same collection representing the Duke of Monmouth ; with that of Oliver Cromwell, at Montagu House, and with an extraordinary little sketch, which we illustrate in colour, by permission of Sir Charles Dilke (Plate IX., No. 1). This also came from Strawberry Hill, where it was bought by the grandfather of its present owner, and it offers a bewildering problem to the student. Walpole declares, in an inscription on the back of it in his own handwriting, that it represents " Miss Temple, Maid of Honour to the Duchess of York, second wife of

Charles Lyttelton," and that it was the work of Gervase Spencer, after an original painted by Cooper, in the possession of Lord Lyttelton, and Walpole ought to have known what he was talking about. It is quite possible that he is correct, but the original portrait from which this sketch is said to have been made is not now in the possession of the Lyttelton family, and the miniature itself bears such a striking resemblance to the work of Cooper that it is difficult to believe that it is a copy by anyone at all. We know how constantly Cooper's work was copied, one of the finest examples of such repetition being the well-known work at Montagu House by Mrs. Ross, a portrait of the Duke of Monmouth, but there is no example known to us of an eighteenth-century painter copying the work of Cooper with the exception of this one, if Walpole's statement is correct. Another curious circumstance about the inscription is that Walpole has made an error in the name. It was not Charles but Thomas Lyttelton who married Christian Temple. She was the daughter of Sir Richard Temple of Stowe, and the heir of Viscount Cobham ; thus it was through her that the Viscounty and Barony of Cobham came to the family.

As we have already written very fully in another place, we are quite unable to accept the series of unfinished miniatures at the Victoria and Albert Museum as being the work of Cooper. There is no external evidence whatever in favour of the tradition. They are painted on a very smooth cardboard, quite a different material to that used by Cooper, and on the back of one of the portraits is an inscription in the same handwriting as is the one on the copy by Mrs. Ross at Montagu House, and apparently signed by the same person. It is quite possible that in the collection the portrait of Lord Brooke (which was not contained in the pocket-book when the original purchase was made) may be a genuine work by Cooper, very likely acquired by Mrs. Ross, as a guide for her own work, but all the other portraits are, we are convinced, the work of this clever copyist, and must not be attributed to the master himself. In the course of our investigations concerning a missing portrait by Cooper, representing the Countess of Exeter, we came upon two interesting letters in the Duke of Rutland's collection at Belvoir Castle, which proved that this portrait was never finished. On the 9th April, 1672, Mr. Charles Manners wrote to Lord Roos in the following terms :—" I haesten on Mr. Cooper all I can to the finishing of my Lady Exester's picture, and hee will surely doe it, God willing ; but at the present the King and the Duke have put severall things into his hands which take him off from all else." Then again, on the 4th May, Mr. Manners wrote again

12

to Lord Roos respecting the same portrait, and he then stated that although Mr. Cooper had promised " with all imaginable respect and kindeness to finish it out of hand, and actually begun it, he just then fell dangerously sicke, and confyned to his bed, and I very much feare hee cannot possibly outlive three days." As a matter of fact, Cooper did not live a day after this letter had been sent, for from Mary Beale's diary we have the information that he died on the 5th May, the diarist writing as follows :—" Sunday, May 5th, 1672, Mr. Samuel Cooper, the most famous limner of the world for a face, dyed." The two letters from which these quotations are taken are to be found in facsimile in the catalogue of Mr. Pierpont Morgan's collection of miniatures. Other odd facts concerning this great painter we learn from Pepys and certain contemporary records. We know that he was an excellent musician, playing well on the lute, and a clever linguist, speaking French with ease. He resided in Henrietta Street, Covent Garden, and frequented the Covent Garden coffee-house ; he was a short, stout man of a ruddy countenance, was married and had one daughter. The Duke of Portland's collection at Welbeck contains the portrait of his wife Christina, and in another collection there is a portrait of his daughter, both fine paintings by the master himself. Christina Cooper was a Miss Turner, and her other sister, Edith, married the father of Alexander Pope. Mrs. Cooper was Pope's godmother and taught him his letters, and to her godson she bequeathed a " painted china dish with a silver pot and a dish to set it in," as well as the reversion of her books, pictures and medals, with Samuel Cooper's " grinding stone and muller," and some of his portrait sketches.

It is not quite certain that Cooper was born in England ; we know the date of his birth, 1609, but we have no certain evidence that he was an Englishman by birth, although there is every probability that this was the case. He was, however, for a while in France, and he was certainly in Holland, and possibly in Sweden also, where his brother, Alexander Cooper, also spent some time. It was in Sweden that we were able to discover a good deal of information respecting Alexander Cooper, and notably a statement concerning his account for certain royal portraits in his own handwriting. Samuel Cooper's appearance is known to us by the portraits in the Victoria and Albert Museum, but an even more interesting sketch of him is in the Pierpont Morgan collection, painted in sepia, on a piece of paper which has been twice folded. An inscription, which we believe to be in his own handwriting, is at the back of a portrait at Welbeck Abbey, and is to the effect that the picture in question, and one or two previous ones, were

13

done for a Mr. Graham, but had not been paid for at the time the artist was writing.

There is hardly a miniature by this eminent man which is not worth careful consideration, and in the power of delineating character and setting before us the actual feelings of his sitters, Cooper had no rival, while one of the great features of his work is its amazing variety. Moreover, the manner in which he adapted his technique, his colour scheme, and his ideas of composition to the special circumstances of the person whom he had to delineate, is very remarkable. His portraits of men are perhaps more attractive than those of women, although he was well able to convey the fascination of a woman's face ; but the strong, rugged men of his period were portrayed by him with quite extraordinary power, and he created a method of portraiture entirely his own, and filled it with individual characteristics. Two splendid examples are amongst our illustrations in colour (Plate VIII.), *Lady Fauconberg* and *Colonel Lilburne*, both from the collection of Mr. Hodgkins.

Of his contemporaries it will suffice to mention one or two, and perhaps the best of them was David des Granges, whose work is represented in our illustrations in colour by a portrait of *Rachel Fane, Countess of Bath*, from the collection of Mr. Hodgkins (Plate IX., No. 2). Of this artist and his parentage we know a little, thanks to the researches of Mr. Lionel Cust in the registers of the Huguenot Church in London. It seems probable that Des Granges, although baptised in the Huguenot faith, did not continue in that communion, because in 1649 he is mentioned in some papers belonging to the French Dominicans as a Catholic, and he was a very close friend of the celebrated artist Inigo Jones, who was also a Catholic. The portrait of the architect by David des Granges, representing Inigo Jones at the age of 68, is at Welbeck Abbey, signed with the initials D.D.G., and is one of the best works by him with which we are acquainted.

For the works of Faithorne or Loggan, Flatman or Lens, we must refer our readers to more elaborate books on miniature painting, and hasten forward towards the eighteenth century. Before we do so, however, it may be of interest that we should refer to an illustration in colour of a miniature which has not hitherto been represented in any book on this subject. It is a portrait which has been bequeathed through various owners as a likeness of *John Milton* (Plate X.), and there is a good deal of evidence to support this very interesting attribution. It came from the Woodcock family, who state that it has been handed down in direct succession from Catherine Woodcock, whom Milton married as his second wife on the 12th of November 1656. She

14

was the daughter of a Captain Woodcock, of Hackney, and the former owners of the miniature stated that their family home was in Hackney. Mrs. Milton had a baby girl on October 19th, 1657, and she and her child died in February 1658, when the miniature was given to her niece, who is stated to have been present at the confinement, and from her it came to its late owners, who only parted with it when actually compelled so to do. It therefore belonged to the Mrs. Milton who is immortalised by the poet in his twenty-third sonnet, where he speaks of her as

> " My late espousèd saint,
> Brought to me like Alcestis from the grave,"

And adds

> ".   .   .   once more I trust to have
> Full sight of her in Heaven without restraint."

He says she

> " Came vested all in white, pure as her mind
> Her face was veiled ; yet to my fancied sight
> Love, sweetness, goodness, in her person shined
> So clear, as in no face with more delight.
> But, oh ! as to embrace me she inclined,
> I waked, she fled, and day brought back my night."

If, as seems most probable, the attribution of this portrait is correct, it gives us a view of Milton at a period of his life of which we have no other portrait, for it must have been painted when he was about 48, and it bears out Aubrey's remarks about him, in which he speaks of his reddish hair, of his " exceeding fayre complexion," of his oval face, and tells us that he was " a spare man." Apparently it was never engraved, and Deborah Milton seems to have known nothing about it, but as she was quite a child when her father's second wife died, and as the portrait passed away from the Milton family so quickly, it is very natural that we should have no other record of it than the miniature itself.

We now come to the eighteenth century, and without referring in detail to the men who preceded the foundation of the Royal Academy, would just mention one of the prominent miniature painters of the early days of the century, Christian Richter by name. He was the son of a Swedish silversmith who came to England in the time of Queen Anne, and settled down with his brother, who was a medallist and a die-sinker. His work is luminous and distinguished, marked by rather an excessive brilliance of red in the carnations, but by a very handsome colour scheme as a rule ; the example we give in our colour plates, the portrait of *Prince*

15

George of Denmark, the consort of Queen Anne (Plate XI.) from the Hodgkins collection, setting forth his characteristics in a satisfactory fashion.

The catalogues of the Royal Academy are full of the names of miniature painters. The period of its foundation was prolific in the number of limners it produced. Miniature painting was the fashion. There were half-a-dozen important painters, and two or three hundred lesser men. The greater men stand out distinctly. Of the lesser men, many are only names to us. Here and there we have scraps of information respecting their history, details concerning the place where they resided, a few dates, and now and again an inscription on the back of a miniature to guide us; but of the vast majority of those who exhibited at the early exhibitions we know little, and of many of them it is not necessary that we should know very much, as their work was neither especially remarkable, nor especially praiseworthy. In considering this period, however, one comment must be made. As a rule, each painter was individual and characteristic. He allowed the personal equation to take an important part in his work, and when the expert is once familiar with the characteristics of the painter, his miniatures can be found quite readily whether signed or not. It is this special personal quality which distinguishes the painters of the period from the host of miniature painters of the present day who have striven to revivify the art, but who in many cases have become mere copyists, and have not allowed personal characteristics to distinguish their work. With the names of the great painters many are familiar, Cosway, Plimer, Smart, Ozias Humphry, Engleheart, Edridge, and Grimaldi are all well known, and the collector is more or less familiar with the names of a few of the minor painters whose works are worth collecting, as, for example, Nathaniel and Horace Hone, Vaslet, and others. There is neither opportunity nor need, in an essay of this sort, to refer to them in detail, because we are not concerned here with anything more than a broad survey of the miniature art, and must not confine our attention to England only. The painters of the eighteenth century offer a sharp contrast to those of the seventeenth, and comparison only makes the contrast the more evident. In the work of Cooper we have strength, power, dignity; in that of Cosway and of the artists of his period is refinement, dexterity, fascination, a spice of flippancy and at times a certain meretricious quality, but this latter is far less seen in Cosway himself than in the work of his followers and admirers. The public demanded something quite different from the artists of the eighteenth century from that which they asked of the earlier school; the work had to be done more quickly, and it must be more charming, sensitive,

16

and radiant. In his skill for giving his sitters exactly what they wanted, and in setting forth on the ivory the dainty grace of the women of the eighteenth century, there was no one who could approach within measurable distance of Cosway himself ; and there is a marvellous fascination about his exquisite work, an individuality which belongs exactly to the period and represents it in all its grace, lightness and flippancy.

Undoubtedly the nearest in merit to Cosway was Andrew Plimer, and some of his works are fascinating in their beauty, but in charm they are never equal to those of Cosway, and the peculiar mannerisms of the artist prevent them from being altogether satisfactory. Plimer had very little power of composition, and he invariably over-accentuated the eyes of his sitters, and constantly repeated a favourite pose either of head or figure, while the extraordinary wiry manner in which he delineated the hair marks out his work at once. Quite as noticeable is his affection for the appearance of his own daughters, and the very shape of their necks and brilliance of their eyes can be seen repeated over and over again in his portraits of other sitters. Less than most of his contemporaries was he able to break away from a strong personal characteristic ; and eventually it became a species of obsession with him, so that his female portraits strikingly resemble one another.

John Smart was a painter of a different type, serious, solid, painstaking. His facial modelling is extraordinary in its accuracy, and his works, like those of Engleheart, appear to have been preferred by the more serious persons in society, whereas those of Cosway and Plimer were particularly appreciated by the gay and frivolous ladies of the Court circle, whose sun and centre was the Prince Regent.

There are miniatures by Cosway which are of pre-eminent beauty, so lightly and with such exquisite skill are they floated upon the ivory. The quality of the material had, of course, an intimate connection with the art of the painter. The seventeenth-century artists knew nothing of the brilliant surface of ivory, although it is possible that one at least of them had an inkling that a more luminous material than vellum, cardboard, or chicken-skin, could be found. There are two miniatures in existence, one of which is in the possession of the author of these pages, the work of Cooper, which are not painted on any of the materials usually adopted by him. This latter is painted on what was at first thought to be a piece of ivory, but microscopic investigation has revealed the fact that it is polished mutton-bone, and the painter has so altered his technique to adapt it to this curious experiment, that for the first moment one would hardly believe the miniature to be by

b

Cooper at all. Its pedigree is, however, unassailable, and a closer investigation reveals many of the master's characteristics, but it is painted with a very fine brush, quite different to the usual broad, full sweep of his work, and it stands out as an interesting experiment on the part of the great painter, who was searching for some material more suitable for a particular style of work. Ivory was not employed until the time of William III., and it seems probable that one of the Lens family was the first to make use of it; but, once adopted, its use became very general, and in the prolific period of the eighteenth century, almost universal.

Cosway is said to have experimented in enamel, and certainly one enamel portrait, with his initials, is in existence. He drew very skilfully on paper, and a few of his miniatures are on that material. One of his works, signed and dated, is on silk, but all these were only experiments, and the greater number of his miniatures are on ivory, which material lends itself perfectly to his craft. In our opinion the finest miniature Cosway ever produced was his unfinished sketch of *Madame du Barry*, one of the greatest treasures of Mr. Pierpont Morgan's collection, and by his kind permission illustrated here in monotone (Plate XII.). It was painted in 1791 on the occasion when Madame du Barry came over to England to recover her jewels, and on her third visit to this country in that year. From this portrait a stipple engraving was made by Condé in 1794, but the miniature itself came into the possession of the Vernons, having belonged to a Miss Caroline Vernon who was maid of honour to Queen Charlotte. It was sold in London in 1902, when it passed to its present owner, and in grace, sweetness, and fascination, is unrivalled, even amongst his wonderful treasures.

Another delightful portrait from the same collection represents the oft-painted *Henrietta, Lady Duncannon*, who was afterwards Countess of Bessborough (Plate XIV., No. 2). She was sister to Georgiana, Duchess of Devonshire, and seems to have spent a great deal of her time in sitting for her portrait, all the artists of the day having painted her. This miniature is remarkable for the fact that it still remains in its original frame, a very magnificent one, richly set with superb diamonds.

Yet another charming portrait by Cosway (Plate XIV., No. 1) came from the Truro collection to Mr. Morgan. It represents *Lady Augusta Murray*, the daughter of Lord Dunmore, who became the wife of the Duke of Sussex, the 6th son of George III. It was her marriage which, although twice performed, in Rome and at St. George's, Hanover Square, was declared null and void under the Royal Marriage Act (12 Geo. III. cap. 11). Her daughter was

Lady Truro. Lady Augusta was only painted twice, and on both occasions by Cosway.

Our coloured illustrations include three portraits of women by Cosway, *Viscountess St. Asaph* (Plate XIII.), the *Countess of Rochford* (Plate XV.) and *Princess Charlotte* (Plate XVI.), all of them distinguished by Cosway's special method of painting the hair, and marked by that inimitable grace in which he excelled.

We also illustrate from Lord Hothfield's collection one of Cosway's more serious portraits of men, *The Earl of Thanet* (Plate XVII.), set upon the usual blue cloudy background, in this instance a trifle paler than usual, and painted with convincing force in a very remarkable colour scheme.

Of the work of the more sedate painters, Smart and Engleheart, we are able to give many characteristic examples. From Lord Hothfield's collection come a splendid pair—*Mr. and Mrs. Percival* (Plate XIX.), painted with that striking force which marks the best work of Smart, upon his usual greenish-grey background, and with very subtle but well-marked modelling in the features. His carnations were ever a little brick-dusty in tint, and he delighted in the ruddier tones of the face, but in depicting the shadows he had few rivals. Although there may be perhaps a certain want of inspiration in his somewhat quaker-like method of work, and in the very low tone of his colouring, yet there is an honesty and a straightforward quality about it which is very attractive, and perhaps that was the reason why Cosway in the words of praise he gave to a painter so different from himself, spoke of him as " honest John Smart."

Engleheart's work has a certain resemblance to that of Reynolds, and the devotion which Engleheart felt towards the President of the Academy had an evidently strong effect upon his own art. He copied Sir Joshua's works over and over again, and gradually a good deal of the influence of the great master permeated the work of his follower. His miniatures were nobler, broader, and far better set upon the oval of the ivory than were those of many of his contemporaries, his draughtsmanship was excellent, and there was a brilliance about his painting of the eyes which is particularly attractive. The large portrait of *Earl Beauchamp* (Plate XX.), from the collection of Lady Maria Ponsonby, is a fine specimen of his best work ; but those of *Mrs. Sainthill* and *Mr. Brundish*, from the collection of Lord Hothfield (Plate XXII.), are good examples of his smaller miniatures, possessing a great deal of charm and delightful in colour. His portrait of *Miss Mary Berry*, from Mr. Pierpont Morgan's collection (Plate XXI.), is quite one of his finest portraits of women. He painted both these sisters, and for a long time the two portraits were in one case, facing one another, but they have now been separated, and lie side by side

b 2

19

in the cabinet. The two ladies were well known as being the close friends of Horace Walpole, who treated them with the greatest tenderness and affection, addressed to them many of his most brilliant letters, and persuaded them to settle down near him at Strawberry Hill. To them he dedicated his catalogue of treasures, and bequeathed a considerable sum of money, and his works and letters were, after his death, edited by Mary Berry, one of the sisters, who lived down till 1852, and died at the advanced age of ninety. From the same collection we have selected two delightful works by Smart, those representing *Sir Charles Oakeley* and a lady whose name is unknown (Plate XVIII.), both distinguished by the elaboration of flesh tints, so quietly and so accurately applied.

The very brilliant, if somewhat flashy, work of Andrew Plimer is particularly well represented in Mr. Pierpont Morgan's famous collection, because it includes the notable series representing Rebecca, Lady Northwick, and her three daughters, all of which are given in our monotone illustrations (Plates XXIII. and XXIV.). Plimer was an adept at flattery, and in this particular case the mother looks hardly older than her daughters, and the three girls are so much alike that one has to look exceedingly closely to notice the position of the band round the head, or of the curl which falls upon the neck, before one girl can be distinguished from another. The same unfortunate mannerism belonging to this clever painter can be seen in *The Three Sisters Ellis*, brilliant works by Andrew Plimer from the collection of Lord Hothfield, and here illustrated in colour (Plate XXV.). When closely regarded it is quite evident that the three girls are very different from one another, but at the first glance we almost wonder how their parents could have known them apart. The painter himself has been led to make little changes in their costume in order that each girl's identity should be preserved, and our remark respecting the exaggeration of the eyes is exemplified in these three very beautiful portraits. By the same painter is the charming representation of *Selina Plimer*, the artist's youngest child, from the collection of the writer of this essay (Plate XXVI.). This miniature came from Plimer's own portfolio, and bears his handwriting upon it. It is very graceful and light in its treatment. The Rushout girls form the subject of the largest painting ever executed by Plimer. His well-known group showing these three girls in one miniature now belongs to Mr. George J. Gould, and is fully described in the life of Andrew Plimer.

In Lord Hothfield's collection, however, is an interesting sketch (Plate XXVII.), a group of the three sisters, evidently his first idea, quite different both in composition and in execution to the finished picture. It came from Plimer's studio, is unmistakably his work, and particularly interesting as a fresh and original idea, even more charming in many ways than the finished picture. In the latter, the girls dress their hair quite differently to what they had it in the sketch, and very possibly the *esquisse* was made on their first visit to the studio, as they stood together that the artist might get an idea of how they looked. Another example of Plimer's work illustrated here in colour is from the same collection, and represents *Mrs. Bailey* (Plate XXVIII.). It is a pleasing picture, though the curious wiriness of hair to which we have drawn attention is very noticeable in it. One of the prettiest pictures that Plimer ever painted of a child is the one which we illustrate in reduced size from the collection of Lady Maria Ponsonby (Plate XXIX., No. 1.) It represents *Sir Charles Kent as a Boy*, playing upon a drum, and is a bright, piquant little picture.

Nathaniel Plimer's work is rarer than that of his brother, and we know very little indeed of the history of the artist. He was a curiously unequal painter. There were times when he could paint far better than his brother, but there are not perhaps more than two or three of his miniatures to which this high praise can be given. His general work is pleasing and agreeable, but does not betoken extraordinary skill. One of the best of his ordinary miniatures is in Lord Hothfield's collection (Plate XXIX., No. 2), and represents *Mrs. Dawes*. It is dated 1798, and is quite a fine picture, but not equal in high merit to two works by this master in the late Mr. Salting's collection, the finest examples of Nathaniel's work we have yet seen.

Ozias Humphry was a greater man than Plimer, but his work in miniature is rare. His draughtsmanship was exceedingly good, his colouring quiet and restrained, and his technique so elaborate, with such fine stipple work, that it has a general resemblance to that of enamel, but differs from this latter because it is not hard in its execution; and there is, moreover, an atmospheric quality about it very attractive. One of Humphry's peculiarities is to be noticed in the elongated shape he gave to the eyes of his sitters, what has been well termed "a greyhound eye," affording a marked contrast to the exceedingly round, over-bold eye, which Plimer was so fond of accentuating. Humphry drew children exquisitely, and his portrait of the *Duchess of Albany* as a child (Plate XXX., No. 1), in the possession of Lord Hothfield, is one of the most delightful miniatures with which we are acquainted. In it his accuracy of draughtsmanship is seen to perfection, and the modelling on the face is so dainty and delicate that the miniature is quite a little gem full of life and vivacity, while the child is represented with a demure, amused look, which is refreshing and natural. There is

21

a very interesting history connected with this miniature. It was painted in Rome in 1773, when Humphry was there with Romney, and it eventually belonged to Horace Walpole, and was in his collection at Strawberry Hill. He is said to have received it from Sir Horace Mann, his great friend and correspondent, who was watching Prince Charles Edward (*de jure* Charles III.), on behalf of the English Government. The other Humphry, which we illustrate from the same collection, represents the *Countess of Thanet* (Plate XXX., No. 2), and is an excellent example of the manner in which Ozias painted a noble lady of a quiet, studious character. The colour scheme in this, again, is very pleasing.

Time would fail to describe the host of minor men who exhibited at the Academy, and it would be impossible to illustrate works by even the chief of them. We have selected just a few; first, an example of the work of John Smart the younger, who is especially well known for his fine pencil work, and for some wonderful copies from drawings by Holbein. There are very few of his miniatures in existence; and the one of *Lieutenant Lygon* (Plate XXXI.), in the collection of Lady Maria Ponsonby which is signed and dated, is a good, natural, life-like portrait, well drawn and composed. Then we would refer to Nathaniel Hone, who was an interesting person, and deserves to be remembered because he was the first artist in the eighteenth century to have what we now call a " one-man show." There is not a great deal of credit belonging to him for this adventure, because, had he not been a very sensitive and passionate man, and painted a picture which annoyed the Academy, the one-man show would never have come off.

In a painting called " The Conjuror " Hone was considered to have made an attack upon the President and upon Angelica Kauffman. It was rejected by the Academy, and in 1775 Hone opened his exhibition at 70, St. Martin's Lane, issued a catalogue, to which he affixed a preface, telling the story of his discomfiture from his own point of view, and appealing to the people respecting the merits of his paintings. The result was not particularly satisfactory, because it was felt that he had been in the wrong. The catalogue is a very rare one, and the whole story is rather interesting in its details.

A fine portrait by Horace Hone, the elder son of Nathaniel, representing William Pitt is in the collection of Lady Maria Ponsonby, and appears in our coloured illustrations (Plate XXXII., No. 2). Horace Hone was a better painter than his father. He excelled in enamel work, and his finest portraits are in that medium. He had a fine sense of colour and loved rich effects of velvet brocade,

22

satin, or fur. Another of his miniatures is in Lord Hothfield's collection, and represents *Lady Mary Nugent;* it is signed and dated, and the owner has kindly permitted us to illustrate it in these pages (Plate XXXII., No. 1).

Yet another miniature from Lord Hothfield's collection illustrates the work of Vaslet (Plate XXXIII.,), of whom we know hardly anything, save that he lived in York and Bath and that he was a clever worker in pastel. He seems to have visited Oxford in 1779, 1780, and 1789, and there is a good collection of his pastel portraits on paper in the Warden's Lodge at Merton College, the portraits carefully signed and dated ; on the majority of them the artist calls himself as L. Vaslet of Bath. There are other collectors in Oxford who have specimens of his work in pastel, but in miniature his paintings are very rare. They are distinguished by a cloudy, flocculent appearance, very much resembling pastel work, and making it evident that the artist was more at home in the use of that material than he was in water-colour.

Our very brief survey of English miniature work must end with Sir George Hayter, by whom we illustrate a portrait of the *Countess of Jersey,* from the collection of Lady Maria Ponsonby (Plate XXXIV.). He was portrait painter to Princess Charlotte and Prince Leopold of Saxe-Coburg, but is better known for his historical paintings than for portraits, and he is almost the last of the nineteenth century miniature painters whose work possesses any special attraction. After his time and that of his contemporaries Sir William Ross, J. D. Engleheart, Robertson, Newton, and Thorburn, the art of miniature painting died away until its revival in recent times.

The painters who worked in enamel occupy a section of miniature work apart, although in many instances the best known enamellers painted portraits also on ivory or on vellum, but they are especially known for their works in enamel. There is little need for us here to do more than define enamel work as a vitreous glaze attached by fusion to a metallic ground, but only those who have attempted to paint portraits in enamel can have any idea of the enormous difficulty of this method of portraiture when fine results are desired. Of all the men who were successful in this most complicated process, Jean Petitot stands out supreme, and his portraits, as a rule excessively minute in size, are distinguished by a delicacy of detail, marvellous in its microscopic exactitude. When it is remembered that the colours were painted on to the panel of gold in the form of a powder, only slightly mingled with a medium, that they did not represent by their tint the colour they were to present when fused, and that the slightest error in the fusing would ruin the plate and cause the colours to run into one another,

23

the marvel is but enhanced when the exquisite works produced by this incomparable artist are examined. The specimen from Mr. Ward Usher's collection (Plate XXXV.), which is illustrated in colour, is a good example of Petitot's portrait of *Louis XIV*. He painted the face of "*Le Roi Soleil*" so often that he must have become familiar with every detail of it, and there is hardly any collection of his works which cannot boast of one of these wonderful little enamels. The story of the painter himself is of considerable interest, and the details of his religious difficulties and of his return to Geneva are well set forth in a book about him written by E. Stroehlin, and published in Geneva in 1905 ; while some further special information more recently discovered can be found in an article by the writer of this essay in the "Nineteenth Century" for January 1908. He left behind him a wonderful little pocket-book containing his own and his wife's portraits, and a narrative of part of his career, written by him in beautiful handwriting. His own portrait belongs to the Earl of Dartrey, and there are some wonderful examples of his work in the Louvre; but the best of his portraits are in England, and there is no collection to rival that of South Kensington in this respect. Perhaps his most extraordinary work is the box belonging to Mr. Alfred de Rothschild, which has fourteen portraits upon it ; but his largest, with one exception, is that of *Mary, Duchess of Richmond and Lenox*, which we illustrate from Mr. Pierpont Morgan's collection (Plate XXXVI., No. 2). It is signed and dated 1643 and is $5\frac{1}{2}$ inches square, the only miniature exceeding it in size being that at Chatsworth, representing the Countess of Southampton, and dated 1642. The latter is, however, unfortunately damaged, whereas the one in Mr. Pierpont Morgan's collection is quite perfect. With these two exceptions, almost all Petitot's miniatures are exceedingly tiny in size. The only other enameller whose work we illustrate was named Prieur, and he married, as her second husband, Marie, the only sister of Jean Petitot. Prieur was a wanderer; we find his work in Poland, Denmark, Russia, Spain, and especially in Denmark, where there are many of his portraits, and where he is believed to have died in 1677. He visited England charged with commissions from the King of Denmark, and, while there, painted a portrait of Charles II. and another of Lady Castlemaine, both from Cooper's miniatures. He was also responsible for a portrait of *Charles I.* (Plate XXXVI., No. 1), but whether contemporary or not we cannot say, for so little is known of Prieur's history, that he may have visited England before 1669, when we know he came over to paint Charles II. In all probability, however, this delightful work, which now belongs to Mr. Pierpont Morgan, is a copy by Prieur from the portrait of the King by

24

Vandyck. Prieur executed several delightful enamel badges for the Danish Orders, and appears to have been in high repute at the courts both of Frederik III. and Christian V.

We have now to deal briefly with the long range of foreign miniature painters, the chief of whom were resident in France, although not always natives of that country. There was a regular tradition of miniature painting in France, extending from the times of the Clouets down to those of the great painters Isabey and Augustin. The works by Jean Clouet were, of course, more of the nature of paintings in manuscripts, and if we are accurate in attributing one of the great gems of Mr. Morgan's collection to Jean Clouet himself, it adds one to the only other seven portraits which have been, with any amount of accuracy, given to this painter. All of the seven are illustrations in one manuscript volume, and probably this eighth was either executed for the same purpose, or has actually been removed from a contemporary work of that kind. When we come to the later Clouets, François especially, we have actual miniatures, and in several instances the drawings for the portraits exist, also enabling us to identify whom the miniatures represent. It would be impossible within the limits of this short essay to deal with all those who succeeded the sixteenth-century men, and we have to make a big jump to the eighteenth century, because it was during that time that the most notable of the French miniature painters flourished, and their works are by far the most important.

Nattier began as a miniature painter, and his mother painted miniatures, and is said to have taught him his art. Later on, he became a well-known portrait painter, but speculating in the wild schemes of John Law, lost his fortune, and a good many of his friends. Once he took up with miniature painting to re-introduce himself to the clients he had lost when he neglected art for the excitement of finance, then dropped it again, and confined his attention down to the time of his death to portrait painting. We illustrate a delightful portrait of *Madame Dupin* (Plate XXXVII., No. 1), the wife of a writer on finance, whose book was suppressed by the order of Madame de Pompadour; but we remember the fair lady who is set forth in this portrait more by reason of the fact that Rousseau was at one time her secretary, and was very much attached to her. The portrait shows her in the hey-day of beauty.

By Hall, the Swede, who lived in Paris, and is generally regarded as a Frenchman, we illustrate a portrait of the *Countess Sophie Potoçki* (Plate XXXVII., No. 2), the celebrated Greek beauty, who became a member of one of the noblest families of the Polish aristocracy. Her story is a strange one. She was born

25

of Greek parents at Constantinople, purchased as a slave by the Russian general De Witte, who made her his mistress; but one night, losing a considerable sum of money at cards, when playing against Count Felix Potoçki, he received an offer from his opponent to waive all claims if the Russian general would pass over his slave to Count Felix. The offer was accepted, and Sophie Clavona became the property of the Polish Count, who was already deeply in love with her. Despite the expostulations of his friends, he promptly made her his second wife, and they lived happily together for many years, while her heritage of beauty has been handed down through succeeding generations. Her portrait was painted over and over again, and the example of it which we illustrate remained for a long time in the private gallery of the family at Warsaw, together with a replica which is still there. It was finally sold to a French dealer, from whom it passed into the hands of its present owner. The famous beauty is in a deep red costume, which wonderfully sets off the charm of her countenance. Another work by Hall from the same famous collection (Plate XXXVII., No. 3) represents the ill-fated *Princesse de Lamballe*, " beauty, goodness and virtue personified, but all her goodness and gentleness could not soften the hearts of those inhuman tigers who immolated her on the altar of Equality." Few scenes are more pitiable than that of the execution of this beautiful woman. She had never committed any action which could have incurred the hatred of the people, but she was the friend of the Queen, and the possessor of considerable wealth; reasons enough to bring upon her head the wrath of the tyrants who preached freedom to France. This miniature is particularly charming in its domestic quality. Madame de Lamballe is shown in her room, engaged in making a wreath of flowers, and every detail concerning her occupation, and the room in which she is seated, is delightfully rendered; but the whole composition is kept so well in hand that the details do not obtrude, nor in any way draw aside the attention from the fair countenance of the lady herself.

The work of Pierre Pasquier is very rare, and not a single example of it is to be seen in the Louvre. He was born in 1731, and died in 1806. He worked largely in enamel, and a great many of his portraits appear on the wonderful snuff-boxes which were given to ministers or eminent diplomatists. Several of them are in Russia. He was distinguished by an unerring perfection of draughts-manship, and this is especially set forth in his profile portraits, one of which, signed and dated, we illustrate from Mr. Morgan's collection (Plate XXXVIII., No. 2). It is probably the finest example of Pasquier's work in existence, and is little more than a sketch in black on ivory, with a steel-blue background, the ivory being left clear where the portrait appears. We do not know who it represents, but it was probably a study for an enamel left incomplete. It is dated 1786, and in its rigid economy of line, exquisite low-toned scheme of colour, and perfection of drawing, occupies an exceedingly high place in miniature painting, and leaves us only regretful that we are ignorant of the name of the sitter.

The example we illustrate of the miniature work of Fragonard must also be anonymous (Plate XXXVIII., No. 1). It is a boy's portrait, and has been said, with a certain amount of evidence, to represent one of his own sons, it certainly does resemble a sketch of one of Fragonard's children, which the artist has named, but not sufficiently for us to be sure respecting the accuracy of the attribution. No one, however, but Fragonard could have painted it, the colour is so daintily placed upon the ivory as to give the effect of having been wafted upon the material, and resting upon it with a feathery lightness. There is generally a good deal of yellow in Fragonard's portraits, or else the colour scheme is mainly grey and white, and this portrait belongs to the second division we have mentioned. It is very pleasing, the face of a quiet, thoughtful child, charmingly represented, and a good example of the work of one of the greatest decorators France ever knew. Fragonard's miniatures are rare, we may add, very rare, and probably no one has such a collection of them as is to be found in the cabinets of Mr. Pierpont Morgan.

By Garriot, a painter who was born in 1811 at Toulouse, studied at Madrid, and painted in Geneva, we illustrate from Mr. Pierpont Morgan's collection a portrait of the *Marquise de Villette* (Plate XXXIX., No. 2), better known as "Belle et Bonne," who was practically adopted as a daughter by Voltaire, and married to the Marquis de Villette at midnight, in November 1777, in the great man's chapel of Ferney, her six uncles being present on the occasion. Ferney had belonged to her and her six uncles, and Voltaire was the means of reclaiming it from the possession of certain of his neighbours into whose hands it had illegally passed in 1761. It was in the arms of "Belle et Bonne" that Voltaire passed away on the 30th of May 1778, when he was eighty-four years old.

A very interesting miniature from the same collection is the one representing a granddaughter of Nattier the artist, painted by Louis Sicardi (Plate XXXIX., No. 1), one of the best miniaturists of the time of Louis XVI. Sicardi painted for over fifty years, produced a great many delightful works, and was responsible for the decoration and portraits that, set upon gold snuff-boxes, were such favourite presents at the French Court.

The two greatest, however, of the painters of the French school were Isabey and Augustin, and Isabey, who was born in 1767, forms a curious link between the eighteenth and the twentieth centuries. He painted Marie Antoinette, Buonaparte, the King of Rome, and the Empress Marie Louise; he also worked for Louis XVIII., received high distinctions from Charles X. and from Louis Philippe, and was appointed Commander of the Legion of Honour by Napoleon III.: moreover, he had a long conversation with the Empress Eugénie (who is still living) in 1854, the year in which he died at the advanced age of eighty-eight. He exhibited between 1793 and 1841, painting portraits of all the eminent persons in France during his long career. Of his earlier work we exhibit in colour two charming companion miniatures from the collection of Mr. Ward Usher, representing the *Empress Josephine*, and the *Empress Marie Louise* (Plate XL.), while of his later, somewhat more florid work, almost invariably distinguished by the presence of a light gauzy scarf which he wound about his sitter, and which he painted to perfection, we give two portraits, one a portrait of *Catherine, Countess Beauchamp*, from the collection of Lady Maria Ponsonby (Plate XLI.), and the other depicting *Fürstin Katharina Bagration Shawronska* (Plate XLII.), from the collection of Fürst Franz Auersperg.

One of the loveliest miniatures Isabey ever painted is that representing *Queen Hortense and her son Napoleon III.*, in the collection of Mr. J. Pierpont Morgan. It contains autograph information in the Emperor's handwriting attesting to its history, and is a lovely example of Isabey's easy, graceful, pleasing work. It is illustrated on Plate XLIII.

An interesting feature of some of Isabey's miniatures is the fact that he worked in conjunction with two Dutch artists, the brothers Van Spaendonck. They were expert painters of flowers and fruit, often employed at the Sévres porcelain factories, one of them being as well a professor of natural history and lecturer on flowers in Paris, and the author of one or two books on flowers and flower-painting. There are several examples of the work of Isabey in which one or other of these brothers has supplied the floral decoration, or a group of fruit in the background.

We now come to Jean Baptiste Jacques Augustin, one of the noblest of the miniature painters of France. He was born in 1759, upon the same day, although separated from him by an interval of ten years, as that on which the great Napoleon, whose portrait Augustin was afterwards to paint, came into the world. He came over to Paris as quite a boy, and lived in a house in that city to which he returned many years afterwards, bringing with him a bride,

28

and where, as a married man, he resided for a considerable time. For a while he found life a hard struggle, but his rare merit soon brought him many clients, and from about 1790 onward until the close of his life, he seems to have had a succession of sitters, including all the notabilities of the day. He left behind him a wonderful collection of sketches, contained in various books, and a large number of unfinished miniatures. Some few years ago the members of the family, in whose possession this great collection had remained, desirous of portioning off two of their daughters, offered the collection for sale. The Directors of the Louvre very much desired to purchase it, as it included many works of great importance, but the whole collection passed into the hands of Mr. Pierpont Morgan, and fills one entire cabinet, giving a view of this artist's work altogether unrivalled. The illustrations which we give are of Augustin's later work rather than those of the early years, although with them is included a brilliant unfinished sketch, representing *The Father of Madame Seguin* (Plate XLIV., No. 2). The one from Mr. Ward Usher's collection represented in colour is a portrait of *Madame Récamier* (Plate XLV.), that from Mr. Morgan's collection in monotone, the famous *Madame de Boufflers* (Plate XLIV., No. 1), the friend of David Hume, who introduced the historian to J. J. Rousseau, and is so frequently alluded to in Horace Walpole's letters. When she fled from France, Madame de Boufflers resided for some time in or near London, and Walpole spoke of her as the most agreeable and sensible woman he ever saw, but he was greatly amused at her want of appreciation of his house. She had never seen a printing press until she came to Strawberry Hill, and Walpole arranged that on the occasion of her visit his private press should print a few lines of French poetry in her praise. In one of his gossipy letters we are told that Madame de Boufflers informed Lord Onslow of the birth of Lord Salisbury two hours after his mother had come from the Opera House, and that from Lord Onslow Walpole himself heard the news.

Of E. W. Thompson, an Englishman, who spent very much of his time in France, and is regarded by the French critics almost as one of themselves, we know very little, but the *Princess de Lieven*, whose portrait he painted (Plate XLIII.), was one of the great ladies of Europe in the nineteenth century. She was a personal friend of Count Metternich and afterwards of Guizot, and Madame de Lieven kept up a steady correspondence with both these statesmen, and exercised, without doubt, a very considerable influence upon European politics.

Two artists of Italian parentage deserve mention, especially as we are able to illustrate, by the permission of their owner, Mr. Ward Usher, delightfully signed examples of their work. By Costa we show an interesting portrait of *Marie Antoinette* (Plate XLVI.) which came from the Bentinck-Hawkins collection; and by Anguissola, the favourite miniature painter to the court of the great Napoleon, we illustrate, in reduced size, a fine portrait of the Emperor's sister, *Princess Pauline Borghese* (Plate XLVII.).

Special attention has been given in our illustrations to the work of the great Viennese miniature painter Füger, because very little is known of his work in England, and there are so few examples of it to be found in English collections. The Viennese collectors seem determined that all the finest works by Füger shall remain in their own city, and they are prepared to give high prices in order that they may carry out this desire. One of the chief collectors in Vienna is Dr. Figdor, and he has been exceedingly kind in allowing many miniatures from his collection to be illustrated for the purpose of this essay, amongst them, five by Füger, perhaps a rather large proportion; but it has been felt that, as the work of the painter is so little known in England, it was well in our illustrations to err on the right side, and give several examples of his delightful workmanship. For a long time the details of his life were buried in obscurity, and all sorts of mistakes were made respecting his work, which was confused with that of other painters, and in some instances not recognised at all. It was not until 1905, when Herr Doktor Ferdinand Laban published a very important article upon him, that Füger's true position was apparent, and Dr. Laban was able from family records to set right the errors of those writers, amongst whom we must include ourselves, who had gone astray from lack of the very material Dr. Laban was able to discover. Since then, Herr Eduard Leisching has added considerably to our information in a splendid book he published on Austrian miniature painters, and he has discovered many more examples of Füger's work, who can now be justly recognised as the greatest of the Continental eighteenth-century miniaturists. He has been called the Viennese Cosway, but the work of Füger has very little affinity with that of our English painter. It is far stronger and more severe, and his more graceful portraits are richer in their colour scheme, and far more elaborate in their decorative effect than anything ever painted by Cosway. There are two wonderful miniatures by Füger in Mr. Pierpont Morgan's collection, one representing three sisters, the Countesses Thun-Hohenstein, and the other Madame Rousbaeck, a lady-in-waiting to the Empress Marie Theresa, but Dr. Figdor's illustrations set forth in excellent manner both the strength and the charm of this wonderful painter. Nothing can be more forcible than the sketch of *Prince Hohenlohe* (Plate XLVIII.), and we realise the power and dignity of the

30

sitter when we regard this marvellous delineation of character. For dainty grace it is difficult to excel the portrait of the anonymous lady (Plate XLIX.), for strength and gracious dignity that of the *Empress Maria* (Plate L.), while the portrait of *Marie Theresia, Countess von Dietrichstein* (Plate LI.) is that of a noble dignified lady of high position, splendid courage, and great charm, and that of *Princess Anna Liechtenstein* (Plate LII.) shows us a thoughtful, learned, and musical lady, a portrait very decorative in colour scheme, and charmingly set upon its oval of ivory.

Another painter whose work was exceedingly popular in Vienna, was Giovanni Battista de Lampi, an Italian born near Trent in 1751, a man very little known outside the narrow limits of the Viennese collectors. He was a wanderer for a few years, painting in Verona, and moving on until he reached St. Petersburg, but when in 1783 he came to Vienna, he was received with open arms, was welcomed by the court and the nobility to such an extent that practically for the rest of his life he resided either in Vienna, or in various towns of Poland from which he could easily reach the capital itself. It was in Vienna that he died at the age of eighty, universally respected and greatly beloved. His wife's portrait is in the gallery at Innsbrück, one of three replicas. The original Lampi retained for himself. His two sons each had replicas, and the remaining one went to his granddaughter, the Baroness Hell, who left it to the museum. One of the replicas which came into the possession of his sons is now a great treasure in Mr. Pierpont Morgan's collection. The portrait from that of Dr. Figdor, which we illustrate in colour, represents Lampi himself (Plate LIII.), and is not only a fine example of the artist's work, serious, and almost solemn in its aspect, but also peculiarly interesting as showing us what the painter himself was like.

Another Viennese miniature painter whose work we illustrate is Moritz Michael Daffinger, who has been called the Austrian Isabey, but these comparisons, like that applied to Füger, are of little significance. What is of special interest with regard to Daffinger is the fact that he adopted the manner of Sir Thomas Lawrence as his own. Lawrence visited Vienna in 1814, and was received with great honour. While there he painted some portraits. Daffinger admired his work immensely, and undoubtedly some of his best miniatures are reminiscent of Lawrence. Especially is this the case with a beautiful girl's portrait from the collection of another Viennese collector, Gräfin Emma Wilczek-Emo-Capodilista ; and for permission to illustrate this delightful miniature (Plate LIV.) we are particularly grateful, as it is a

31

charming specimen of the best work of the nineteenth century, a pleasing portrait, and very agreeable in its colour scheme.

Daffinger had many pupils, and one of them, Emanuel Peter, exceeded all the rest in skill. We illustrate two clever portraits by him (Plate LV.), from Dr. Figdor's collection, in which the ladies are wearing very decorative head-dresses. It is suggested that the two fair sitters were relatives, probably cousins, and were painted for some exceptional occasion, perhaps a masquerade, as the custom to wear fantastic head-dresses for such special entertainments still prevails in Vienna.

Finally we must mention Ferdinand Georg Waldmüller, whose own portrait by himself appears on Plate LVI. He was one of Lampi's pupils, but, like Daffinger, a profound admirer of Sir Thomas Lawrence. His early days were one continual struggle, and he earned his living by painting bon-bon boxes, and by giving lessons in drawing in girls' schools, until his skill was recognised and he had won a position for himself in Vienna. He even went on the stage in a travelling troupe with his beautiful wife, who was an actress, but forced the attention of critics by his splendid portrait studies, and at length was appointed curator of the Lamberg Gallery, became a popular portrait painter, and died in 1865 justly esteemed for his skill and ability.

Our survey of this fascinating art of the miniature painter has necessarily been brief. There is still a good deal of information to be gathered up concerning the eighteenth-century artists, and probably some of their descendants possess papers and records of vast interest, hidden away amongst family treasures. Perchance this essay may encourage some of them to make the necessary search, and so add to the information available on the lives and careers, especially of our English miniature painters.

Of the earlier men there is not much chance of obtaining new information now, but there is always a possibility that letters or sketches by such a painter as Cooper may again come to light, and if such so fortunate a circumstance were to take place we should delight to learn more of the greatest of our British miniature painters, whose portraits were for so many years ignored in favour of the more brilliant, but far less important, works of the painters who exhibited in the early days of the Royal Academy.

GEORGE C. WILLIAMSON.

PLATE I

MRS. PEMBERTON
BY HANS HOLBEIN

PLATE II

QUEEN ELIZABETH
BY NICHOLAS HILLIARD

PLATE III

PHILIP II., KING OF SPAIN
BY ISAAC OLIVER

MARY, QUEEN OF SCOTS
BY NICHOLAS HILLIARD

QUEEN ANNE OF DENMARK
BY ISAAC OLIVER

ALL FROM THE COLLECTION OF MR. J. PIERPONT MORGAN

PLATE IV

A SON OF SIR KENELM DIGBY
BY ISAAC OLIVER (1632)

FREDERICK, KING OF BOHEMIA
BY ISAAC OLIVER

THE QUEEN OF BOHEMIA
BY ISAAC OLIVER

PLATE V

THE DUKE OF BUCKINGHAM
BY JOHN HOSKINS, THE ELDER

PLATE VI

QUEEN HENRIETTA MARIA
BY JOHN HOSKINS, THE ELDER

PLATE VII

CHARLES II
BY SAMUEL COOPER

JOHN, EARL OF LOUDOUN
(1598-1662)
BY SAMUEL COOPER

BOTH FROM THE COLLECTION OF MR. J. PIERPONT MORGAN

PLATE VIII

COLONEL LILBURNE
(1618-1657)
BY SAMUEL COOPER

VISCOUNTESS FAUCONBERG, DAUGHTER OF OLIVER CROMWELL
BY SAMUEL COOPER

BOTH FROM THE COLLECTION OF MR. E. M. HODGKINS

PLATE IX

MISS CHRISTIAN TEMPLE
BY OR AFTER SAMUEL COOPER

FROM THE COLLECTION OF THE RT. HON. SIR CHARLES DILKE, BART., M.P.

RACHEL FANE, COUNTESS OF BATH AND LATER OF MIDDLESEX
(1612-1680)
BY DAVID DES GRANGES

FROM THE COLLECTION OF MR. E. M. HODGKINS

PLATE X

JOHN MILTON
ARTIST UNKNOWN

PLATE XI

GEORGE, PRINCE OF DENMARK
BY CHRISTIAN RICHTER

PLATE XII

MADAME DU BARRY
(1746–1793)
BY RICHARD COSWAY. R.A.

PLATE XIII

VISCOUNTESS ST. ASAPH (*NÉE* LADY CHARLOTTE PERCY) SECOND
WIFE OF GEORGE, VISCOUNT ST. ASAPH, AFTERWARDS THIRD
EARL OF ASHBURNHAM
BY RICHARD COSWAY, R.A.

PLATE XIV

LADY AUGUSTA MURRAY
WIFE OF THE DUKE OF SUSSEX
BY RICHARD COSWAY R.A.

HENRIETTA, LADY DUNCANNON
AFTERWARDS COUNTESS OF BESSBOROUGH
(OB. 1821)
BY RICHARD COSWAY R.A.

BOTH FROM THE COLLECTION OF MR. J. PIERPONT MORGAN

PLATE XV

LUCY, WIFE OF WILLIAM H. NASSAU, FOURTH EARL OF ROCHFORD
BY RICHARD COSWAY, R.A.

PLATE XVI

H.R.H. PRINCESS CHARLOTTE OF WALES
(1796-1817)
BY RICHARD COSWAY, R.A.

PLATE XVII

HENRY TUFTON, ELEVENTH AND LAST EARL OF THANET
(1775-1849)
BY RICHARD COSWAY, R.A.

PLATE XVIII

SIR CHARLES OAKELEY
(1751–1826)
BY JOHN SMART

PORTRAIT OF A LADY
(NAME UNKNOWN)
BY JOHN SMART

BOTH FROM THE COLLECTION OF MR. J. PIERPONT MORGAN

PLATE XIX

THE HON. MRS. EDWARD PERCIVAL
BY JOHN SMART

THE HON. EDWARD PERCIVAL, SECOND SON OF JOHN, SECOND EARL OF EGMONT
(1744-1824)
BY JOHN SMART (1801)

BOTH FROM THE COLLECTION OF LORD HOTHFIELD

PLATE XX

EARL BEAUCHAMP
BY GEORGE ENGLEHEART (1805)

PLATE XXI

MISS MARY BERRY
BY GEORGE ENGLEHEART

PLATE XXII

MRS. SAINTHILL
BY GEORGE ENGLEHEART

JOHN JELLIARD BRUNDISH, M.A. SMITH PRIZEMAN AND
SENIOR WRANGLER IN 1773
BY GEORGE ENGLEHEART

BOTH FROM THE COLLECTION OF LORD HOTHFIELD

PLATE XXIII

REBECCA, LADY NORTHWICK
(Ob. 1818)
BY ANDREW PLIMER

PLATE XXIV

THE HON. HARRIET RUSHOUT
(Ob. 1851)
BY ANDREW PLIMER

THE HON. ANNE RUSHOUT
(Ob. 1849)
BY ANDREW PLIMER

THE HON. ELIZABETH RUSHOUT
(Ob. 1862)
BY ANDREW PLIMER

ALL FROM THE COLLECTION OF MR. J. PIERPONT MORGAN

PLATE XXV

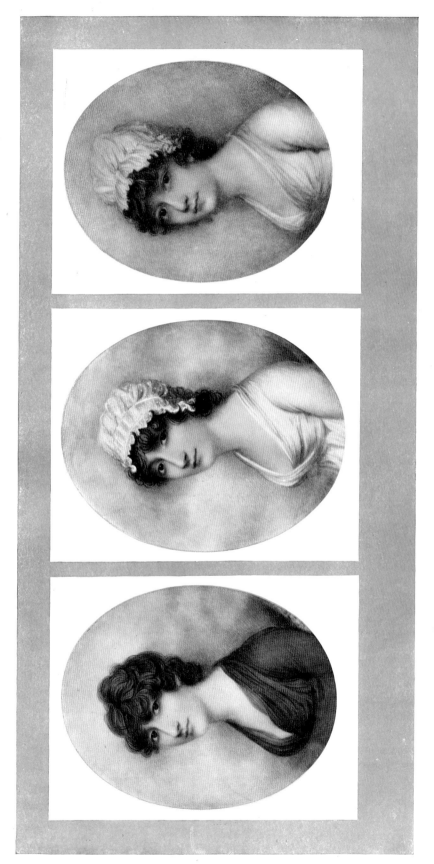

ELIZABETH, MARGARET CAROLINE AND ANTOINETTE, DAUGHTERS OF JOHN ELLIS, ESQ.
OF HURLINGHAM, MIDDLESEX AND JAMAICA
BY ANDREW PLIMER

ALL FROM THE COLLECTION OF LORD HOTHFIELD

PLATE XXVI

SELINA PLIMER
BY ANDREW PLIMER

PLATE XXVII

THE SISTERS RUSHOUT
BY ANDREW PLIMER

FROM THE COLLECTION OF LORD HOTHFIELD

PLATE XXVIII

MRS. BAILEY, WIFE OF LIEUTENANT BAILEY, WHO WAS PRESENT AT THE
STORMING OF SERINGAPATAM IN 1799
BY ANDREW PLIMER

PLATE XXIX

SIR CHARLES KENT, BART., AS A CHILD
BY ANDREW PLIMER (1786)

FROM THE COLLECTION OF LADY MARIA PONSONBY

MRS. DAWES
BY NATHANIEL PLIMER (1798)

FROM THE COLLECTION OF LORD HOTHFIELD

PLATE XXX

CHARLOTTE, DUCHESS OF ALBANY, DAUGHTER OF
CHARLES EDWARD STUART BY CLEMENTINA,
TENTH DAUGHTER OF JOHN WALKENSHAW
(1753-1789)
BY OZIAS HUMPHRY

MARY, WIFE OF THE EIGHTH EARL OF THANET
(OB. 1778)
BY OZIAS HUMPHRY

BOTH FROM THE COLLECTION OF LORD HOTHFIELD

PLATE XXXI

LIEUTENANT LYGON
BY JOHN SMART, JUN. (1803)

PLATE XXXII

LADY MARY ELIZABETH NUGENT, AFTERWARDS MAR-
CHIONESS OF BUCKINGHAM, AND IN HER OWN RIGHT,
BARONESS NUGENT
(OB. 1812)
BY HORACE HONE

FROM THE COLLECTION OF LORD HOTHFIELD

THE RT. HON. WILLLIAM PITT
BY HORACE HONE

FROM THE COLLECTION OF LADY MARIA PONSONBY

PLATE XXXIII

MISS VINCENT
BY VASLET OF BATH

PLATE XXXIV

THE COUNTESS OF JERSEY
BY SIR GEORGE HAYTER (1819)

PLATE XXXV

LOUIS XIV
BY JEAN PETITOT, THE ELDER

PLATE XXXVI

CHARLES I.
BY P. PRIEUR

MARY, DUCHESS OF RICHMOND AND LENOX
(1623-1685)
BY JEAN PETITOT THE ELDER (1643)

PLATE XXXVII

MADAME DUPIN
(OB. 1799)
BY JEAN MARC NATTIER

THE COUNTESS SOPHIE POTOCKI
(OB. 1822)
BY P. A. HALL

LA PRINCESSE DE LAMBALLE
(OB. 1792)
BY P. A. HALL

ALL FROM THE COLLECTION OF MR. J. PIERPONT MORGAN

PLATE XXXVIII

PORTRAIT OF A BOY
(NAME UNKNOWN)
BY JEAN HONORÉ FRAGONARD

PORTRAIT OF A LADY
(NAME UNKNOWN)
BY PIERRE PASQUIER (1786)

BOTH FROM THE COLLECTION OF MR. J. PIERPONT MORGAN

PLATE XXXIX

A GRAND-DAUGHTER OF NATTIER, THE ARTIST
BY LOUIS SICARDI

LA MARQUISE DE VILLETTE
("BELLE ET BONNE")
BY GARRIOT

PLATE XL

THE EMPRESS MARIE LOUISE
BY JEAN BAPTISTE ISABEY

THE EMPRESS JOSEPHINE
BY JEAN BAPTISTE ISABEY

BOTH FROM THE COLLECTION OF MR. J. WARD USHER

PLATE XLI

CATHARINE, COUNTESS BEAUCHAMP
BY JEAN BAPTISTE ISABEY

FROM THE COLLECTION OF LADY MARIA PONSONBY

PLATE XLII

FÜRSTIN KATHARINA BAGRATION SKAWRONSKA
BY JEAN BAPTISTE ISABEY (1812)

PLATE XLIII

QUEEN HORTENSE AND HER SON, AFTERWARDS NAPOLEON III
(1808-1873)
BY JEAN BAPTISTE ISABEY

LA PRINCESSE DE LIEVEN
(NÉE DOROTHY BENCKENDORFF)
(1784-1857)
BY E. W. THOMPSON

BOTH FROM THE COLLECTION OF MR. J. PIERPONT MORGAN

PLATE XLIV

MADAME DE BOUFFLERS
(1725-1800)
BY J. B. JACQUES AUGUSTIN

THE FATHER OF MADAME SEGUIN
BY J. B. JACQUES AUGUSTIN

PLATE XLV

MADAME RÉCAMIER
BY J. B. JACQUES AUGUSTIN

PLATE XLVI

MARIE ANTOINETTE
BY M. V. COSTA

PLATE XLVII

PRINCESS PAULINE BORGHESE
BY B. ANGUISSOLA

PLATE XLVIII

PRINCE FRANZ W. HOHENLOHE
BY HEINRICH FRIEDRICH FÜGER

PLATE XLIX

PORTRAIT OF A LADY—NAME UNKNOWN
BY HEINRICH FRIEDRICH FÜGER (CIRCA 1790)

PLATE L

EMPRESS MARIA THERESIA, SECOND WIFE OF THE EMPEROR FRANCIS I OF AUSTRIA
BY HEINRICH FRIEDRICH FÜGER

PLATE LI

MARIE THERESIA, COUNTESS VON DIETRICHSTEIN
BY HEINRICH FRIEDRICH FÜGER

PLATE LII

FÜRSTIN ANNA LIECHTENSTEIN-KHEVENHÜLLER
BY HEINRICH FRIEDRICH FÜGER (CIRCA 1795)

PLATE LIII

PORTRAIT OF THE ARTIST
BY GIOVANNI BATTISTA DE LAMPI

PLATE LIV

GRÄFIN SOPHIE NARISKINE
BY MORITZ MICHAEL DAFFINGER (CIRCA 1835)

PLATE LV

GRÄFIN SIDONIE POTOCKA—DE LIGNE
BY EMANUEL PETER

PORTRAIT OF A LADY—NAME UNKNOWN
BY EMANUEL PETER

PLATE LVI

PORTRAIT OF THE ARTIST
(1793-1865)
BY FERDINAND GEORG WALDMÜLLER